# EVERYBODY HAS A BELLYBUTTON

## Your Life Before You Were Born

By Laurence Pringle • Illustrated by Clare Wood

BOYDS MILLS PRESS

Text copyright © 1997 by Laurence Pringle
Illustrations © 1997 by Clare Wood

Published by Caroline House
Boyds Mills Press, Inc.
A Highlights Company
815 Church Street
Honesdale, Pennsylvania 18431
Printed in Hong Kong

Publisher Cataloging-in-Publication Data
Pringle, Laurence.
Everyone has a bellybutton : your life before you were born / by Laurence Pringle ; illustrated by Clare Wood.—1st ed.
[32]p. : col.ill. ;  cm.
Summary : A nonfiction book that discusses human life before birth, and hence, why the bellybutton.
ISBN 1-56397-009-0
1. Birth—Children's literature. 2. Human anatomy—Children's literature.
[1. Birth. 2. Body, Human.] I. Wood, Clare, ill. II. Title.
612 [E]—dc20    1997    AC    CIP
Library of Congress Catalog Card Number 95-83168

First edition, 1997
Book designed by Jean Krulis
The text of this book is set in 16-point Garamond Light.
The illustrations are done in pencil and pastels.

10 9 8 7 6 5 4 3 2

*Dedicated with love to my wife, Susan,*

*still nurturing our grown-up babies.*

*—L. P.*

*To the Sorrentino family, with all my love.*

*And to the memory of Jerrad Pikna, a happy, loving soul.*

*—C. W.*

E verybody has a bellybutton. You have one. Your mom and
dad each have one.  Even grandmothers and grandfathers
have bellybuttons.

Whether you call it a bellybutton or a navel, everybody in the world has this special mark in the center of their belly.

Look at your bellybutton. Touch it. This funny little mark is a reminder of an amazing time in your life—when you grew as a baby inside your mother's body.

Everybody begins life as a single cell that is smaller than the period at the end of this sentence. This cell was created when a female egg joined with a male sperm cell. Then, for a few days, it drifted slowly along in a tube within your mother's body.

As it drifted along, the cell split in two. Next those cells split, making four cells. Those four cells also divided and formed eight cells. The cells kept dividing and dividing, forming a round hollow cluster.

Still only a speck, this ball of cells soon drifted into a larger space in your mother's body, called the *uterus* or *womb*.

The cluster of cells settled down in a place on the wall of the uterus. There it was nourished by the uterus and by a spongy organ called the *placenta,* which had developed from the cell cluster.

Another part of the cluster became the first stage of a baby, an *embryo.* You were once an embryo. At first you looked more like a curled-up tadpole than a baby. Your arms and legs were just little buds. Your face wasn't formed yet.

An embryo grows quickly. After only two weeks as an embryo, your heart began to pump blood. If you put your hand near the center of your chest right now you can feel your heart beating. It first began to beat when you were about the size of a pea.

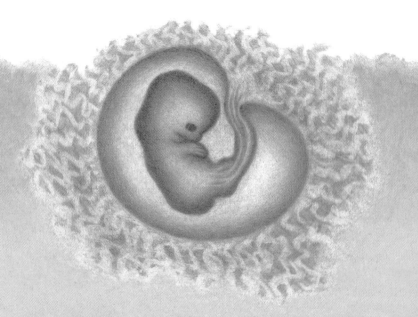

After twenty more days, you tripled in size. Your arms and legs grew longer. Your face began to take shape. You started to move a little bit.

You were a water animal. You floated inside a clear-walled sac filled with fluid. A cord from the placenta came through the sac wall and was attached to the center of your body, right where your bellybutton is now. This strong cord is called an *umbilical cord*.

The umbilical cord was a life line between you and your mother. A big vein in the cord carried blood that brought water, oxygen, and nutrients from your mother's food to you. Two smaller veins in the cord carried away wastes. Everything you needed to thrive and grow came to you through this cord.

You grew each day, and you grew very fast. One day your hands were little paddles. Three days later your fingers had formed.

In just sixty days you grew from one cell to millions of cells. You were still only an inch long, but now you looked like a baby, with fingers and toes, eyes, ears, and nose.

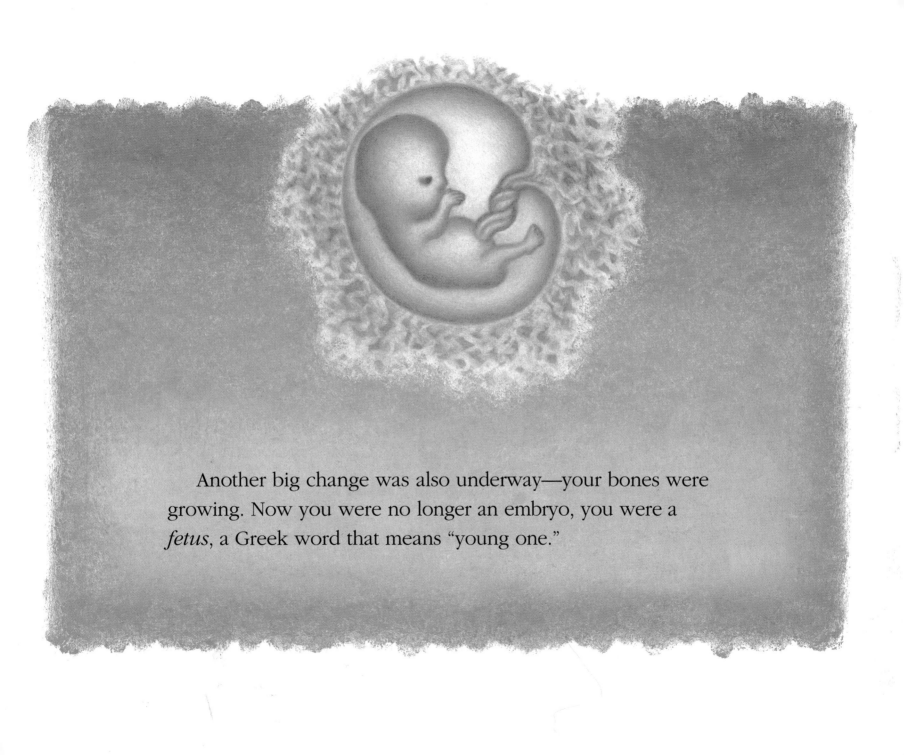

Another big change was also underway—your bones were growing. Now you were no longer an embryo, you were a *fetus*, a Greek word that means "young one."

One day your hand touched your lips, and your mouth started a sucking movement. You began to suck your thumb. From then on you often sucked your thumb, fingers, or hand. You did not know it, but this was practice for when you would take milk from your mother's breasts or a bottle.

As you grew you needed more space in your mother's body. Her belly stretched to make room for you. Then one day, when you were about five months old and ten inches long, your mother felt a faint fluttering movement inside her belly. It was you moving your arms and legs.

From then on your mother and others could sometimes feel you moving about inside. In your watery home you had room to swing your arms, flip from side to side, and even turn somersaults.

You were not ready to be born, though. You had more growing to do.

Your eyelids stayed closed until you were seven months old. Even then you could not see very well. You did not need to see. The womb was dark, except for a faint reddish glow from light that passed through your mother's belly and the wall of the uterus.

You could hear. Mostly you heard nearby sounds, like the murmur of blood rushing through your umbilical cord. Faintly, from beyond your watery world, you could hear your mother's voice. Perhaps you heard music, too.

Sometimes your chest moved, as if you were breathing air in and out, but you were underwater and could not yet breathe. The oxygen you needed came from your mother's lungs. It was carried to all parts of your body in the fresh blood of your umbilical cord. Your lungs were ready, though. You would need them when you were born.

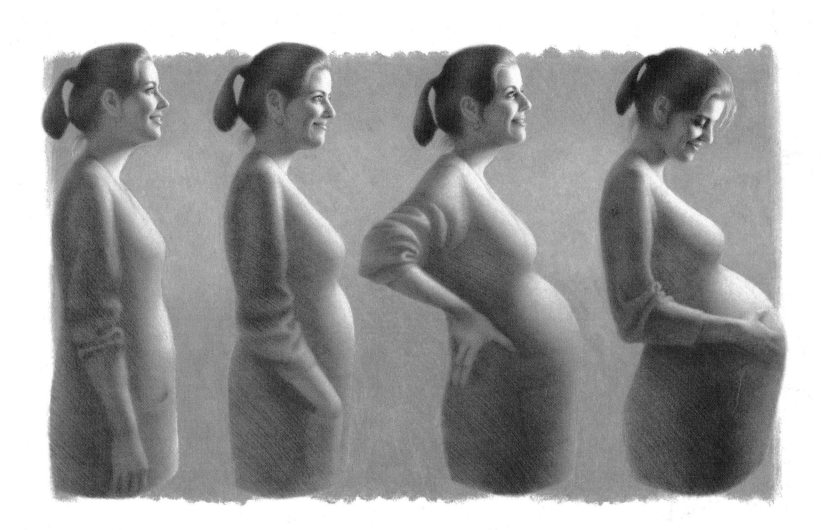

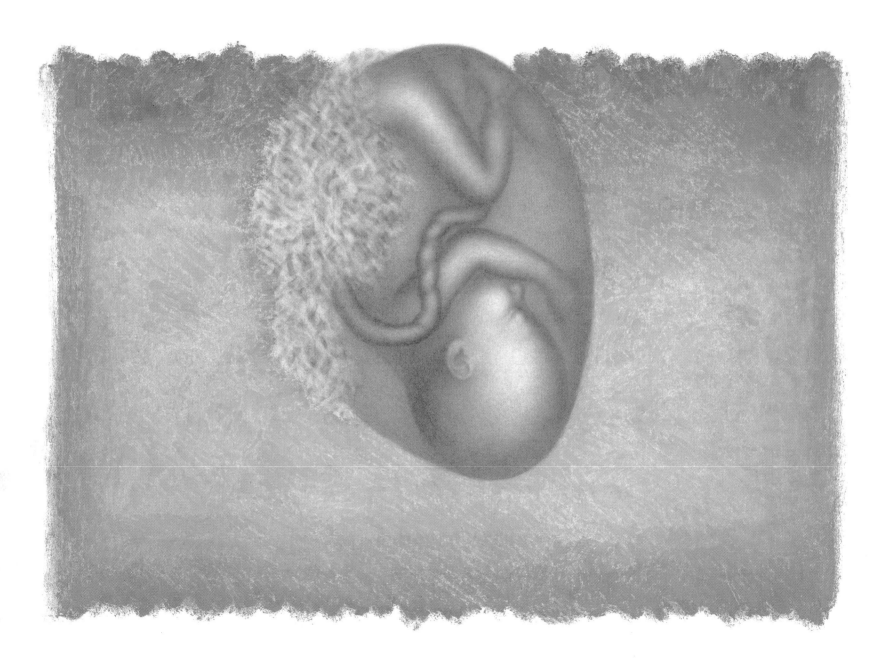

After about 260 days in the dark, warm shelter of your mother's womb, it was nearly time for your birthday. You could hardly move. You weighed about six pounds or more and were about twenty inches long.

Some of the weight you had gained was fat. This would help keep you warm when you left the warmth inside your mother to live in the colder air outside.

You curled up with your knees by your chin. Your head snuggled down at the bottom of your mother's uterus. You were ready to be born.

The muscles at the bottom opening of the uterus relaxed so you could pass through. Then other muscles of the uterus squeezed tightly around you. They relaxed, then tightened again. These were your mother's strongest muscles. One strong squeeze broke the sac of water that surrounded you.

Your mother's muscles squeezed with their greatest power. Bit by bit they pushed you headfirst down through the opening of the uterus and into the birth canal or *vagina*. They pushed you through the vagina, which opened as wide as possible to let you through.

First the top of your head appeared. Your mother's muscles worked even harder. Your head and then your shoulders squeezed through the opening. Then the rest of your body slid easily out into the world.

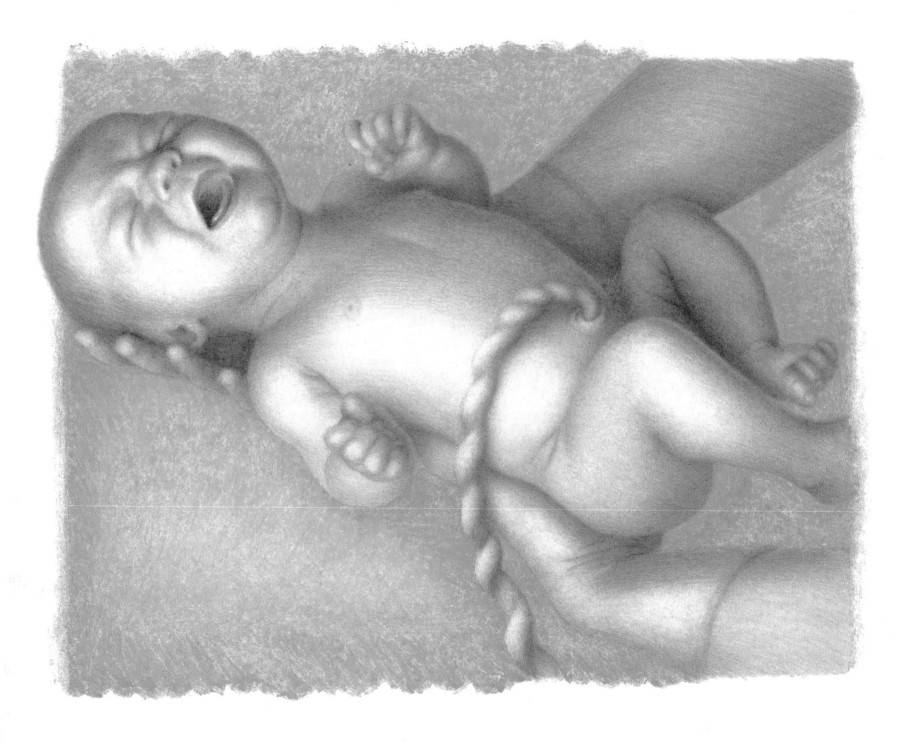

What a shock! You had left a wet, dark, warm place. Now bright lights shone on you. For the first time air touched your skin, and it felt cold.

You took your first breath. Air rushed in to blow up your lungs like little balloons. You breathed air in and out, again and again. Your lungs began to give your body oxygen.

Your umbilical cord was still attached inside your mother, but you did not need it anymore. The doctor cut it and left a little piece sticking out from your belly. The cut did not hurt.

Now you were free of the cord. You could be held by your mother. You could be admired and cuddled by people who loved you.

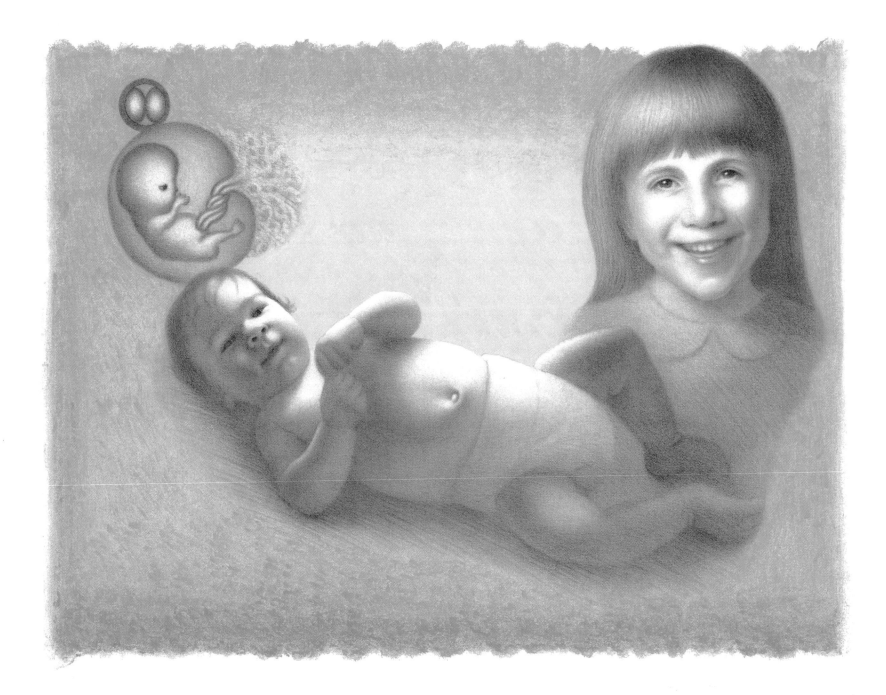

Soon you tasted warm milk for the first time. You began to like life out in the air, with its light, sounds, and people.

In a week or two that little bit of umbilical cord dried up and fell off. All that remained was a special mark right in the center of your belly.

Look at your bellybutton. Touch it. It is a reminder of that amazing time in your life—when you were a tiny embryo and then a fetus, living in a sac of water inside your mother's body, and growing to be you.

## A NOTE TO PARENTS

Children love to learn about that special time in their lives before they were born. As you read this book to your children, they will treasure the details you can add that are unique to them; for example, the time you saw them in an ultrasound image, or the day they as a fetus did a memorable amount of "bouncing around."

You also may want to share other details about a child's development and birth that differ from the process described in this book. For instance, you can tell a child born by Caesarean section a little about that process.

Some young children may not have the patience to listen to the whole book. They will enjoy hearing parts of it and talking with you about the pictures. They are probably fascinated with the subject and may return to it, hungry for more information, when they are older.

By beginning and ending with its focus on the bellybutton, this book empha-sizes the unique physical bond between mother and child. Other mammals also have umbilical cords. With your children you might search for the faint navel scar hidden by hair on the belly of a cat or dog.

This book also emphasizes the nine months of aquatic life that every human experiences within the womb. It says only a little about birth, and even less about how babies are conceived. Young children may not even ask questions about the first step in the reproduction process, but older ones likely will. As surely as everybody has a bellybutton, everyone is also naturally curious about sexuality and how babies are made. Avoid overtelling. Information that is vital for a preteen may be unnecessary for, and even unwanted by, a preschooler.

# FURTHER READING

The books listed below give more details about human reproduction and can help you answer your children's questions.

Flanagan, Geraldine Lux. *The First Nine Months of Life*. New York: Simon and Schuster, 1982.

Hamberger, Lars, with color photographs by Lennart Nilsson. *A Child is Born: The Completely New Edition*. New York: Delacort Press, 1990.

Kitzinger, Sheila, with color photographs by Lennart Nilsson. *Being Born*. New York: Grosset & Dunlap, 1986.

Rugh, Roberts and Landrum Shettles. *From Conception to Birth: The Drama of Life's Beginnings*. New York: HarperCollins, 1971.